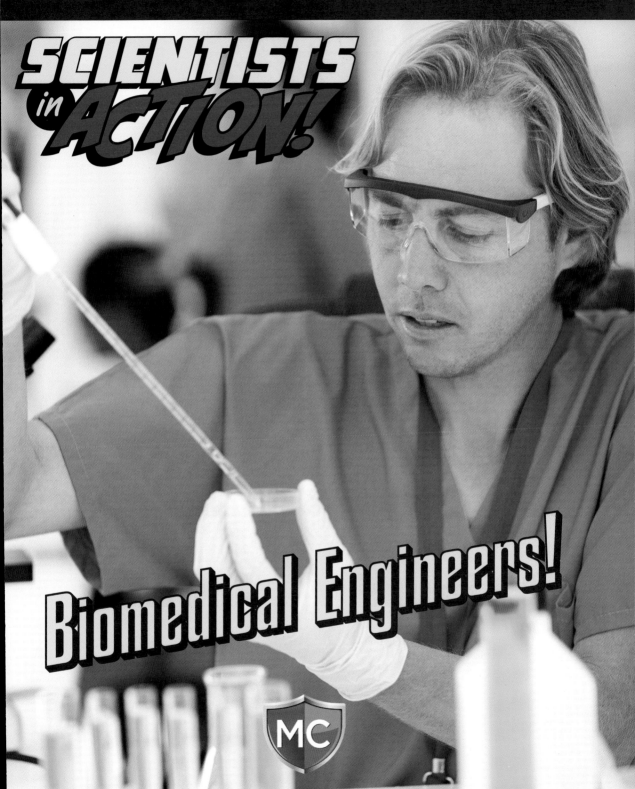

SCIENTISTS in ACTION!

Archaeologists!	Climatologists!
Astronauts!	Crime Scene Techs!
Big-Animal Vets!	Cyber Spy Hunters!
Biomedical Engineers!	Marine Biologists!
Civil Engineers!	Robot Builders!

SCIENTISTS in ACTION!

Biomedical Engineers!

By Diane Bailey

Mason Crest
450 Parkway Drive, Suite D
Broomall, PA 19008
www.masoncrest.com

Printed and bound in the United States of America.

Series ISBN: 978-1-4222-3416-7
Hardback ISBN: 978-1-4222-3420-4
EBook ISBN: 978-1-4222-8481-0

First printing
1 3 5 7 9 8 6 4 2

Produced by Shoreline Publishing Group LLC

Santa Barbara, California
Editorial Director: James Buckley Jr.
Designer: Tom Carling, Carling Design Inc.
Production: Sandy Gordon
www.shorelinepublishing.com

Cover image: Dreamstime.com/Michael Zhang

Library of Congress Cataloging-in-Publication Data
Bailey, Diane, 1966- author.
        Biomedical engineers! / by Diane Bailey.
            pages cm. -- (Scientists in action!)
        Audience: Grades 9-12
        Includes bibliographical references and index.
ISBN 978-1-4222-3420-4 (hardback : alk. paper) -- -- ISBN 978-1-4222-3416-7 (series : alk. paper) -- ISBN
978-1-4222-8481-0 (ebook) 1. Biomedical engineering--Juvenile literature. 2. Biomedical engineers--Juvenile
literature. 3. Medical technology--Juvenile literature. I. Title.
R856.2.B35 2016
610.28--dc23
                                                        2015004675

Contents

Key Icons to Look For

Words to Understand: These words with their easy-to-understand definitions will increase the reader's understanding of the text, while building vocabulary skills.

Sidebars: This boxed material within the main text allows readers to build knowledge, gain insights, explore possibilities, and broaden their perspectives by weaving together additional information to provide realistic and holistic perspectives.

Research Projects: Readers are pointed toward areas of further inquiry connected to each chapter. Suggestions are provided for projects that encourage deeper research and analysis.

Text-Dependent Questions: These questions send the reader back to the text for more careful attention to the evidence presented here.

Series Glossary of Key Terms: This back-of-the-book glossary contains terminology used throughout this series. Words found here increase the reader's ability to read and comprehend higher-level books and articles in this field.

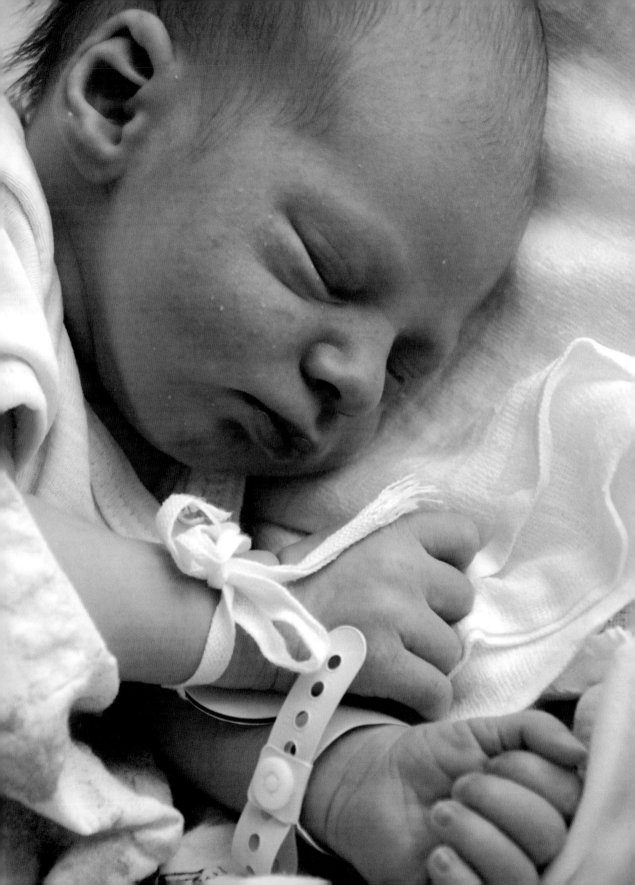

Action!

Kaiba Gionfriddo was only six weeks old when he stopped breathing. His father desperately pushed on his son's small chest, trying to get him some air. They rushed him to the hospital. Fortunately, Kaiba got better, and doctors sent him home.

Then, two days later, the same thing happened. Kaiba's family discovered he had a rare medical condition. His windpipe had not developed properly and was collapsing when he tried to breathe. There was no pathway for air to get into his lungs. Without treatment, he would probably die. His doctors contacted a pair of scientists at the University of Michigan. One was a children's doctor named Glenn Green. The other was Scott Hollister, a biomedical engineer, also known as a BME.

WORDS TO UNDERSTAND

splint a device used to support a body part or keep it still

ventilator a machine that lets a person breathe artificially

The two scientists had been working together to develop a type of **splint** that might solve Kaiba's problem. It could be implanted in the baby's airway and would hold it open so he could breathe. However, the device was still in the experimental stage. It had been tried on animals, but not humans.

Kaiba's situation, though, was an emergency. He needed the splint now. His parents were willing to try anything that might work. Green and Hollister got special permission from the hospital and the Food and Drug Administration (FDA) to try the device on Kaiba. Then they set to work—fast.

The scientists were excited to get to try their technology. They were also nervous. What if something went wrong?

"It was a mixture of elation and, for lack of a better word, terror," Hollister remembered. "When someone drops something like this in your lap and says, 'Look, this might be this kid's only chance'…it's a big step."

There were still several steps to go. The first thing the scientists did was create detailed pictures of Kaiba's lungs. They used an advanced type of X-ray machine called a CT scanner. It takes several pictures and combines them so that the result is similar to a three-dimensional image.

With this precise information, the scientists could design the device to fit Kaiba's body exactly. Next they used computers to create a model of what the splint would look like.

The next part was to actually make it.

The splint was made of a material called PCL, a form of high-tech plastic. It looks like a powder, and can be formed into a lot of different shapes, depending on where it is needed. It's been used in medicine before. For example, it can plug holes in the skull after patients have brain surgery.

The PCL in Kaiba's splint would break down in his body after about three years. His body would absorb it without causing him any harm. By that time, Kaiba's windpipe would have enough time to develop properly. Then he wouldn't need the splint anymore.

To create this experimental splint, the scientists turned to an emerging technology: 3-D printing. A 3-D printer uses computer models to build objects out of plastic such as PCL. These printers can make chess pieces, violins, locks and keys, shoes—even a car! The best part is that a 3-D printer can get the job done fast. That is just what Kaiba needed.

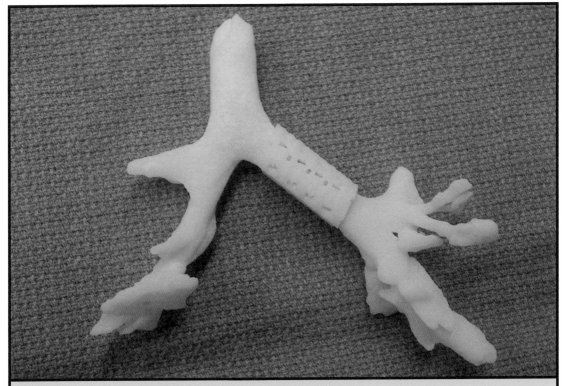

Made of plastic and created by a 3-D printer, this successful use of a splint showed doctors and engineers that individually made body replacement parts might be lifesavers in the near future.

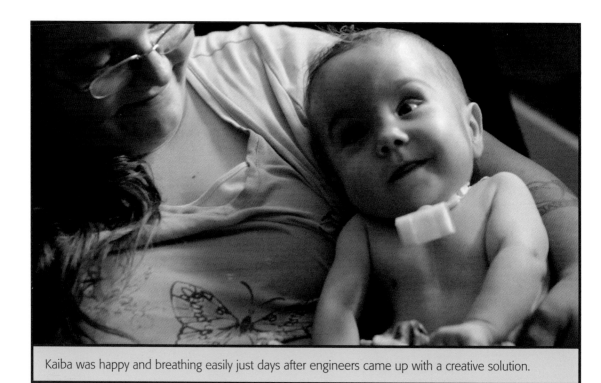

Kaiba was happy and breathing easily just days after engineers came up with a creative solution.

He was in the hospital, attached to a **ventilator** to help him breathe. He did not have much time.

"Printing" a splint takes longer than printing a picture, but within a day, the printer had created the splint that Kaiba would need. It had small ridges on the side, which would help it keep its shape. It looked like a hose for a vacuum cleaner—but much tinier! It was only a few centimeters long and only eight millimeters wide (about a third of an inch). Scott Hollister did not want to take any chances, though.

What if the splint turned out to be the wrong size? What if someone dropped it on the floor during the surgery? To be on the safe side, he printed up several different versions of the splint.

Doctors inserted the splint, and everyone watched anxiously. The results were immediate. Kaiba started breathing on his own!

Kaiba remained on a ventilator for three more weeks, just to make sure everything worked. Then he went home. Soon he was playing with the family's dog and getting into trouble, just like a regular toddler—and he hasn't had any more problems breathing.

Not very long ago, this story might not have had such a happy ending. Biomedical engineers such as Scott Hollister and others, however, have made a lot of progress in the field. Today, people can live longer and better lives thanks to such work.

Being biomedical engineers takes them to one of the most exciting places there is—inside the human body.

The Scientists and Their Science

Engineers design and make things. Medical professionals help people who are sick or injured. When the skills from both of those fields come together, the result is biomedical engineering. Biomedical engineers develop machines and techniques that help with human health.

In fact, BME has been around as long as people have. Humans have always figured out ways to fix things that were broken with their bodies,

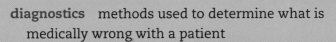

WORDS TO UNDERSTAND

diagnostics   methods used to determine what is medically wrong with a patient

genes   information stored in cells that determines a person's physical characteristics

sensors   things that detect and gather information

vaccine   a method of protecting someone against a disease, delivering medicine using an injection with a needle or to make them feel better. For example, the body of a 3,000-year-old Egyptian woman was found with an artificial toe made out of wood and tied to her body with leather straps.

The field of BME really began to take off in the 1950s. There were huge advancements in medicine and technology. More powerful computers let scientists do complex math problems and run complicated software. Scientists found more ways in which math, engineering, biology, and medicine could overlap. Then they put these skills to work on the problems of the human body.

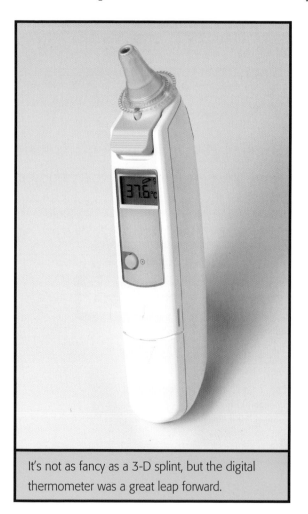

It's not as fancy as a 3-D splint, but the digital thermometer was a great leap forward.

The Three Ds

BMEs work on many kinds of projects. It is helpful to divide that work into three categories. The "three Ds" are devices, **diagnostics**, and drugs. Devices are things that doctors or patients use to perform a certain task. Some familiar devices include X-ray machines or stethoscopes. Many homes have simple devices such as thermometers or blood-pressure machines. These are some early examples of biomedical engineering at work.

In the last 50 years, BMEs have developed more complex devices. One such example is a pacemaker.

Some people have hearts that beat too fast, too slow, or unevenly. If the rhythm is off by too much, it can threaten that person's life. A pacemaker sends out electrical signals that prompt the heart to beat. Artificial limbs and joints are other devices that BMEs work on. Robots that can take the place of some human functions are also a big part of what BMEs are up to today.

Some devices are specially designed to help doctors diagnose a patient to figure out what is wrong. Half a century ago, doctors did not have very many ways to examine what was going on inside a person's body. They could take X-rays, measure blood pressure, and do a few other simple tests. These tools were helpful, but they did not give the full story. Now there are more high-tech ways to "see" inside the body. CT scanners and MRI machines are devices that make images of the inside of the body. Some machines measure levels of chemicals. Others track how cells are moving. Still others record signals being given out by the brain or heart.

Often, patients need drugs to treat illnesses. Some BMEs are experts on cells. They understand the chemical processes that happen inside cells. They also study the physics that make cells move around. With this information, they can work to develop drugs that can interact effectively with the cells.

Miniature Medicine

Nanotechnology is the science of building things with particles that are only a few nanometers wide. How tiny is that? The wire in a paper clip is about one millimeter across—and there are a million nanometers in one millimeter. Products made with nanotechnology can usually only be seen with microscopes. BMEs who work with nanotechnology can actually get inside the body's cells, and even study a person's **genes**.

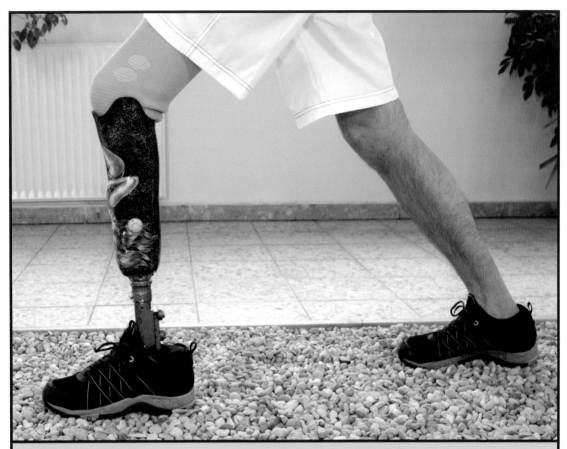

Engineers combine their knowledge of materials, machines, power, and manufacturing with the sciences of anatomy and biology to create remarkably useful and life-changing artificial limbs.

Amazing Accomplishments

*T*he work of BMEs combines science with technology. For example, contact lenses are common today, but they are a BME success story.

Contacts were developed in the 1800s and 1900s. They brought together many branches of science and engineering. First, scientists had to understand the physics of how light is absorbed and reflected. Next, they studied the anatomy of the human eye. This guided them in developing a lens that could fit on it. Finally, they determined what kinds of materials could be used safely on the eye.

If you've never had the mumps or measles, it is probably because you got a **vaccine** against it. Vaccines are used to prevent people from becoming sick with certain diseases, such as polio, chicken pox, or even the flu.

A vaccine is a method of injecting someone with a small amount of bacteria or virus that causes a disease. It is not enough to make someone sick. However, it is enough for the body to recognize that a foreign substance is invading. Then the immune system gets to work. It develops special substances that can fight the infection if the body is exposed to a larger dose. BMEs work to develop vaccines in large doses, then distribute them to many people.

Mumps is a good example of a disease that has been nearly wiped out by vaccine. It hasn't been completely eliminated, but the number of cases has dropped by more than 99 percent since the vaccine first was introduced late in 1967. There were more than 150,000 cases of the mumps reported in the United States in 1968; now there usually are only a few hundred cases each year.

Another exciting aspect of BME is making artificial body parts. Many people have lost fingers, arms, or legs from injuries or disease. Now, they can sometimes get new ones. BMEs who study mechanics figure out how to construct new limbs and joints, and make them move properly. Other specialists make sure these replacement materials work with the body's biology. Still others design **sensors** to go in the artificial limb. These sensors communicate with the brain and tell it how to move the new limb. What the body does naturally takes a whole team of BMEs to re-create.

What It Takes

BMEs-in-training learn about the electronics and machines they will one day use to create new body parts.

Anyone who wants to be a biomedical engineer is in for a lot of school! Biology and engineering classes are standard. Even though the word "biomedical" comes first, it is probably the engineering part that is more important. People who enter this field usually study engineering first. Later, they apply that to medicine.

BMEs also learn physics, math, and computer programming. They may study more specialized subjects, too. For example, they could learn about mechanics, which is how machines work. The human body is one of the most complex machines there is. How do joints move? How does blood flow? Those are the mechanics of the body.

BMEs study engineering and mechanics to help them create products that mimic the mechanics of the body. Depending on what area they want to focus on, BMEs might also study electronics to help them create robotic limbs. Or they can look into materials science. Finding products that do not disrupt the body's natural processes is a key part of any new biomechanically engineered product. They study how plastics are created, what metals can be formed or shaped into parts, and even how to make parts that look like human skin.

Computer programming can be very useful. Many artificial parts connect to computers for some of their functions. A BME who can tell the computer what to do will be ahead of his or her peers.

Life Sciences

For the biological side of their two-part work, BMEs take several important classes in the life sciences. Biology teaches them how bodies work, grow, and change. They learn about all the parts and systems of the body in anatomy classes.

Chemistry class can be a big part of some BMEs' education. The body is a sea of different chemicals. Some of the devices the BMEs will work on have to exist in that sea, so knowing how chemicals react to each other is important.

It's easy to get excited about a new technique or technology, but BMEs must also think about why they are doing the work in the first

It's Not All Science!

Most of a BME's training is related to science and math, but students can't fall asleep in English class, either. Their jobs will require them to write reports about new discoveries and inventions. They will need to write clearly, using scientific language. Knowing a foreign language also is helpful. BME research happens all over the world. In fact, some students take part in exchange programs. Those let them travel to other countries to work. Some BMEs also study law or business so they can bring products to the market.

Understanding chemistry is important for BMEs as they prepare to create devices that will live in the "sea of chemicals" that is the human body.

place. People who need special devices and procedures are often very sick and in pain. BMEs must also be sympathetic to patients and their families, so studying psychology can be helpful.

BMEs pay attention to details. They measure things precisely, and they analyze problems carefully. They even try to think of new problems! Sound weird? Not to James Patton, a BME professor at the University of Illinois. He says, "In research, the most important personal characteristic is to not solve problems, but to conceive of new ones."

There is a lot to learn in engineering, biology, and medicine. More discoveries come every day. It can be hard to keep up. It's important not to get discouraged. Lots of things don't work the first time, but BMEs don't give up. Instead, they go back to the drawing board and try again.

Text-Dependent Questions

1. What are the three Ds of BME?
2. Why is a CT scan better than an X-ray?
3. What non-science skills does a BME use?

Research Project

Be a medical detective! Talk to older people you know, such as your grandparents. Ask them about a medical breakthrough that happened in their lifetime and why it was important.

Tools of the Trade

Biomedical engineers spend a lot of time in their laboratories. Those labs are filled with fancy equipment and materials. Test tubes and microscopes are just the basics. BMEs focus on different areas, so they each need specialized tools.

Robots

Just because the body can't do something itself does not mean it can't be done at all. That's one of the reasons for having robots. A robot is a machine that is programmed to do a certain task. Sometimes a

---

WORDS TO UNDERSTAND

artery a type of blood vessel that carries blood from the heart to parts of the body

compatible able to work together without conflict

stem cell a basic cell that can be grown or developed into a more specific type of cell

transplant to move something (such as an organ) from one place to another

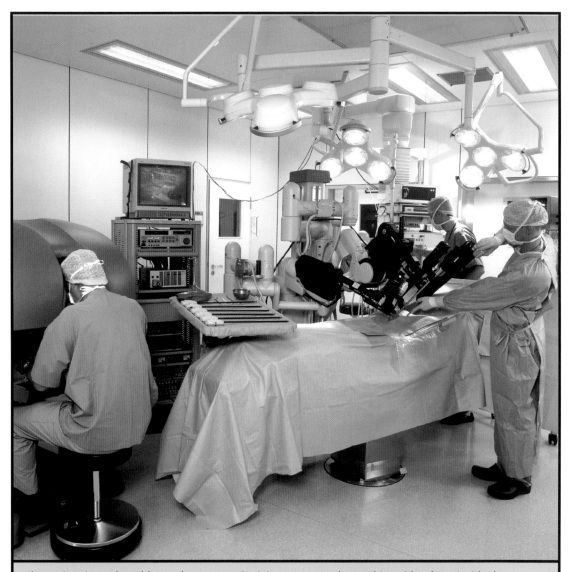

The patient is on the table . . . the surgeon is sitting at a console watching video from inside the patient. The machines over the patient hold the scopes and instruments that the doctor guides.

robot looks like a person, but it does not have to. A robot can be big or small, depending on the type of job it has to do.

BMEs help create a variety of robotic devices. Artificial limbs are one example. They contain sensors that communicate with a computer or even with the human brain. Then they move based on the feedback from the sensors. Other robots are used to help doctors or surgeons. In the past, surgery had to be done by hand. Surgeons needed a sharp knife and a sharper eye. Some procedures were impossible. Doctors could not access the places in the body with the problem, or they did not have tools that were good enough. Today, there are many robotic surgeries that can go where a surgeon's hand cannot. A microbot is a very small robot that can burrow into a person's **artery**. It's equipped with a tiny drill that lets it scrape plaque off the sides of the artery, helping blood to flow more easily.

The Camera Pill

Most cameras are too big to go inside a person's body. However, BMEs have developed tiny cameras that can be inserted into a person without having to cut the person open. There's even a "camera pill." This camera is encased in a tablet, and someone can swallow it. It makes its way down the throat, into the stomach, and through the intestines. It photographs the whole journey. It's completely safe, and at the end of the ride, it comes out the other end along with everything else!

Other robots are being used to replace humans for ordinary jobs. Some robots have a spoon attached to help people feed themselves. Others help patients who need physical therapy. These robots can help patients build up muscles in their arms and legs.

Bioreactors

People need a good environment in which to grow. They need healthy food and nutrients. It's the same for a cell—after all, the body is just one big bag of cells. Cells are delicate. They need exactly the right conditions in which to grow. A bioreactor is a special machine that creates an ideal environment for cells. A bioreactor might be as small as a test tube, or as large as a water-heater tank.

Bioreactors have a lot of sophisticated instruments. Some make sure there are the correct amount of fluids and nutrients. Some regulate the concentration of different gases such as oxygen or carbon dioxide. The bioreactor also keeps the temperature just right—not too hot or too cold.

A **stem cell** is a special kind of cell. It is like a blank page. Scientists can nurture stem cells so they can grow into a specific type of cell, such as skin or bone. It just depends on the environment they are in. A bioreactor can be specially developed to grow just one type of cell, such as blood vessels or muscle tissue. Others are designed to grow bones or skin.

3-D Printers

*N*eed a new liver? How about some replacement skin? Already, the work of BMEs has led to successful **transplant** operations. In a transplant, patients receive a new organ in place of one that has failed. Transplants, however, are complicated and risky. Someday,

BMEs might be able to "print" entire organs, such as a kidney or liver. How? By using a three-dimensional printer. Already, BMEs can use 3-D printers to make more simple body parts, such as blood vessels and veins. Most organs have a lot of veins, so this is an important first step in printing the entire thing. Of course, the splint used to help the baby on page 10 was made with a 3-D printer.

Instead of using paper and ink, 3-D printers use special materials to build things. These could be actual biological material, such as cells. Or they could be nonliving materials, such as certain plastics, that are compatible with the body. The 3-D printer layers the material just as

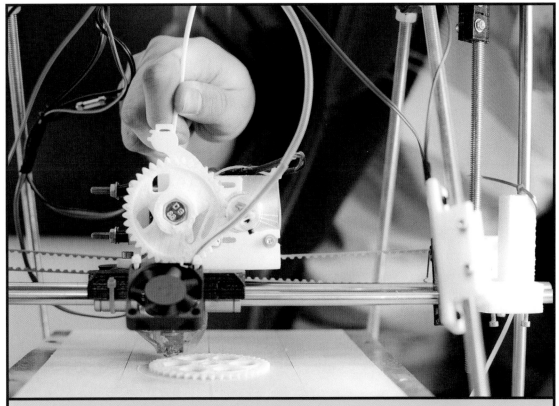

This 3-D printer is creating the white gear at the bottom. It takes instructions fed in by a computer program and builds the object one very small layer at a time.

a regular printer layers ink onto a page. It is kind of like building with blocks, except that these are the building blocks of life.

To build a blood vessel, BMEs first get stem cells from the patient. Then they place them in an incubator to grow more. Special chemicals are added so that the cells will grow into the specific type of cell that is needed. When there are enough, the cells are packed tightly into little pellets. Now it's time for the printing.

Have you ever made shapes out of gelatin? When the gelatin is hot, you can pour it into a mold that is any shape you like. After it cools, it will come out in that shape. That's kind of how printing a blood vessel works. In this case, the printer first squirts out a substance called

The 3-D printer can use several kinds of material. This printer is using a green plastic that feeds in from the reel on the left. The green material then flows through the tubes to the printer head.

hydrogel, which is like a high-tech jelly. This is used to create a mold in the shape of a blood vessel. Next, the cell pellets are loaded into the printer. Then, they are printed into the hydrogel mold.

Where They Work

BMEs work in a variety of environments. Some work in hospitals, operating and maintaining sophisticated equipment. They work closely with patients and doctors, and pass information back to the companies that create the devices and equipment. Other BMEs work at the offices and laboratories of those companies. They might be tasked with creating, designing, and developing new products and devices. Or they might be in charge of making sure that existing products are manufactured accurately.

Still others in this field do research and teach at colleges and universities. Some of the most amazing and groundbreaking discoveries in the field of biomedical engineering comes from the minds of professors and students working side-by-side in and out of class. While companies are looking for things that will make money by helping people, often the work at universities is aimed at education and discovery.

No matter what their office or lab looks like, though, all BMEs are really working in one place: the human body. Their jobs depend on knowing how the body works. What makes things go wrong? How can they help fix it? A BME's workplace can be the brain or the heart. It can be a whole organ or just a single cell. It can be six feet tall, or only a few dozen nanometers.

Humans share some qualities, but in other ways they are different from each other. Each person's individual characteristics are determined by his or her genetics, so some BMEs study how genes work, too.

This engineer is working with a patient to make sure that the prosthetic leg fits perfectly. Like doctors, BMEs often have a hands-on relationship with patients; it's not just working in a lab!

Teaming up with doctors and other BMEs is very important. Sometimes doctors know what the problem is, but they do not know how to fix it. On the other hand, an engineer might be able to solve a problem, but first he has to know what the problem is. Sharing research and knowledge helps BMEs connect the dots. Then they can develop solutions.

 # Text-Dependent Questions

1. Why are stem cells important in BME?
2. Name some conditions that a bioreactor controls.
3. In what environments do BMEs work?

 # Research Project

Build your own bioreactor. Fill a glass bowl with water and add some rocks. Add a little water from a pond or puddle. This is where algae grow. Now add some fish food or a crushed vitamin. In a few days, see if more algae have grown. Experiment with different conditions by raising the temperature of the water or putting the bowl in bright sunlight. What happens?

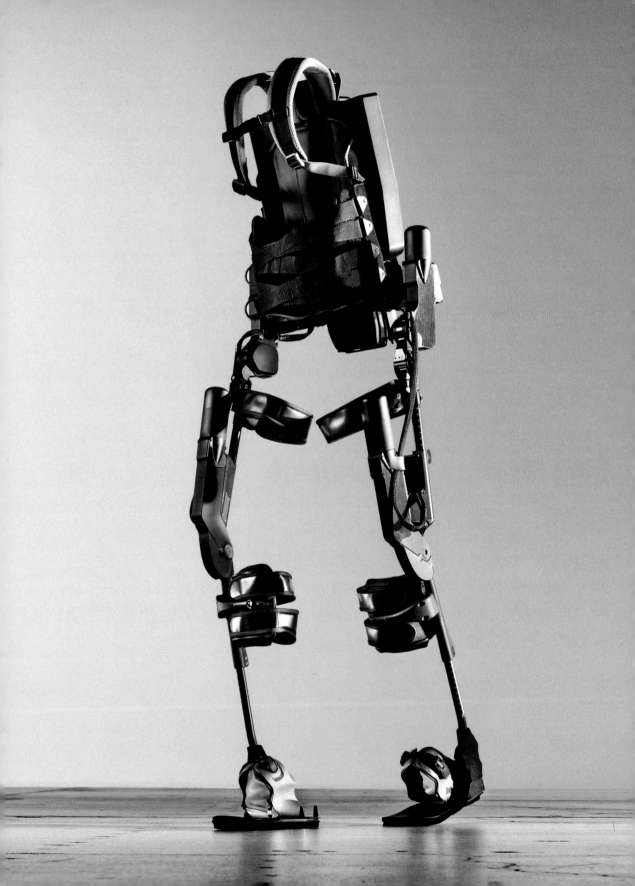

Tales From the Field!

BMEs are curious about every part of the body, inside and out. They want to know how it works, and how they can make it work better. At laboratories all over the world, BMEs are building the things that make people ask, "How did they do that?!"

Walk On

It only takes an instant to damage the human spine so badly it will never work again. The spine is a central piece of the skeleton. Without a working spine, people are **paralyzed**. They cannot walk or move their limbs. Now, though, some of those people are able to move again.

WORDS TO UNDERSTAND

bionic   to be assisted by mechanical movements

exoskeleton   a type of skeleton that fits on the outside of the body

paralyzed   unable to move part or all of the body

retina   the part of the eye that receives visual information and converts it into signals for the brain

This exoskeleton was developed for the military to help soldiers increase their strength and lifting power.

They are getting a new skeleton, but it does not go on the inside of their body. Instead, an **exoskeleton** is a machine shaped like a skeleton, and is worn on the outside.

For most people, the brain sends out signals to take a step forward, and the body does it. Those lines of communication are broken in a paralyzed person. The exoskeleton can help. It has special sensors that pick up signals from the body. Then it kicks into gear to perform the action. In 2014, a paralyzed young man wore an exoskeleton to a soccer game at the World Cup. He was able to make the ceremonial "opening kick."

His suit had several parts. A cap with sensors in it picked up signals from his brain. Then it sent them to a computer that he carried in a backpack. Using electronic code-breaking, the computer interpreted the electrical brain signals, then sent the message along to the man's legs so he could kick the ball.

The suit also had a "skin." Instead of being made out of biological cells, it was constructed from flexible boards loaded with electronic sensors. They measured things such as pressure, speed, and temperature. These signals then were sent to the person's real skin. Information like this is important because it helps the person feel where he is. Are his feet touching the ground? How far apart are they? This information helps the brain send the right signals to know what to do next. "You can't walk without knowing where the floor is," says Miguel Nicolelis, one of the team of scientists who worked on this BME marvel.

Exoskeletons are not just for disabled people. The military has developed suits that will help soldiers. They will give them extra strength so that they can carry more gear. Scientists are working to make suits that are smaller and lighter so they can be worn for longer periods.

A Better Bandage

*I*t's easy to stick on a bandage if you scrape your knee or elbow. If it falls off, you can just put on another. It's a lot harder, though, if the bandage needs to go inside your body! That's exactly what some patients need after they have surgery. Two BMEs at the Massachusetts Institute of Technology (MIT) wanted to create a bandage that would work on internal organs. A bandage could be better than stitches. Stitches sometimes fall out too soon, causing internal blood leaks. A bandage could be safer and easier to use.

The BMEs knew their bandage had to be compatible with the body. It had to be made out of something that would not cause an infection. That's especially important in someone who has just had surgery. The material also had to be made so that the body could soak it into its system after its job was finished. Like a regular bandage, it needed to be flexible and elastic, so that it could stretch. Of course it had to be sticky, too.

Nature has already provided a lot of engineering answers. The scientists looked to the animal world as they worked. They found a strange helper: geckos. These small lizards have uneven feet, with a lot of tiny ridges. They also have millions of toe hairs that let them cling to surfaces. These help geckos crawl up and down walls, and even across ceilings.

First, the BMEs made a special kind of rubber that would work with human biology. Then they molded it so that it was similar to the bottom of a gecko's foot. It had a lot of little hills and valleys. After that, they spread on a type of glue that is made from sugar. The bandage can even stick to wet surfaces. That is important since the inside of the body is all wet!

Keeping Pace

*I*n 1958, Arne Larsson was a very sick man. His heart was not functioning properly. It did not beat about 70 times a minute like it should. Instead, it only beat about 30 times a minute. Mr. Larsson passed out dozens of times a day. His wife, Else Marie, was determined her husband would live. She read in the paper about doctors who had been experimenting with pacemakers that could be put directly into a patient's heart. It would keep the heart beating at the rate it should. Mrs. Larsson went to see the doctors and asked to get a pacemaker for her husband. They told her they had only used the device on animals. There was not one ready for people yet. Mrs. Larsson would not take no for an answer. She said: "So make one!"

The doctors set to work. They scheduled an emergency surgery, but kept it a secret. It was very likely something could go wrong. They didn't want people watching. As it turned out, the surgery worked,

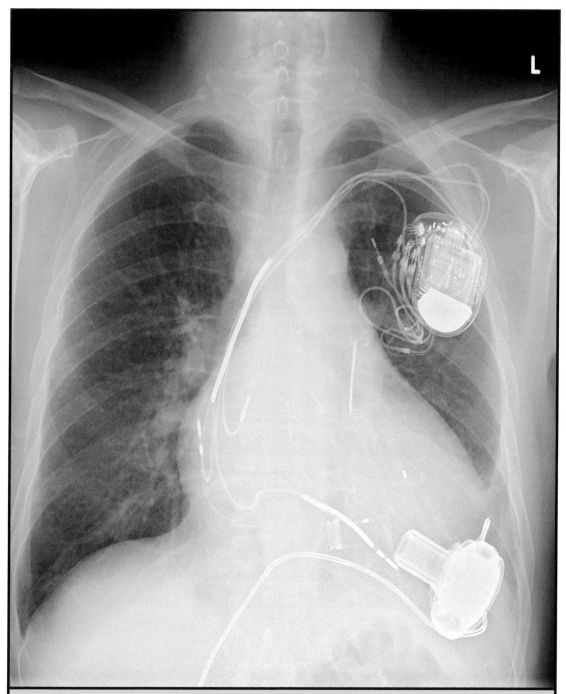

This X-ray of a human chest shows how pacemakers are implanted in the body. The wires lead from the small devices into the heart, ready to send an electric pulse that will keep the heart beating.

A Great Mistake

In 1956, Wilson Greatbatch was building an electronic device to record heart sounds. When he reached into a box to get a part, he accidentally took out the wrong one. When he installed it on his device, it started making pulsing signals. That wouldn't work for his device, but Greatbatch realized he might have discovered something even more important. Those electrical signals sounded just like a heartbeat. By 1958, Greatbatch had developed an internal pacemaker that improved on ones used a few years earlier. His pacemakers were being widely used by the 1960s.

but the pacemaker didn't. It failed after only a few hours. The surgeons were ready for that, though. They put in another one. It lasted a little longer, but still failed after a few days. That was okay, too. Mr. Larsson got another one. In fact, over his lifetime, Mr. Larsson got 26 different pacemakers! He lived until he was 86.

By the 1960s, the pacemaker had become a lifesaver for people with heart problems. In 1983, Dr. Rune Elmqvist was one of the doctors who worked on Mr. Larsson. He later said, "At first I viewed the pacemaker more or less as a technical curiosity. So it was fantastic to see its tremendous development." Today, it remains one of the great achievements in biomedical engineering.

Building Bones

Sometimes, broken bones do not mend. Sometimes, bones do not grow at all. People do not look normal if they do not have proper bone structure. Their skin has nothing to hang onto. Bones also help protect the body's delicate internal organs. People without bones in the right places are more likely to get hurt.

Gordana Vunjak-Novakovic is a BME at Columbia University in New York. She wanted to grow new bones that could help people. Her work began with stem cells. Stem cells can be grown into a variety of different kinds of cells, depending on the conditions in which they develop. The mineral calcium is an important ingredient in bone. When a little extra calcium is fed to growing cells, it triggers them to grow into bone cells.

Vunjak-Novakovic wondered if other factors also influenced the growth of the cells. She had worked with patients in the hospital who had to stay in bed for weeks or months at a time. She noticed that after a while, their bones got weaker. This made her think that maybe

Dr. Vunjak-Novakovic and her team at Columbia created a new way to grow human facial bones using stem cells, a process that could help thousands of people around the world.

developing cells also needed to move around while they were growing. Vunjak-Novakovic decided to test her idea on cartilage, a type of tough tissue that connects bones. As she grew a batch of cartilage, she occasionally rotated it so that it was in a different position. The result was just what she had hoped. That cartilage was much stronger than the cartilage that stayed still. Vunjak-Novakovic went on to invent a device that gently presses down on growing stem cells, just as the body's joints would. This makes them stronger.

Vunjak-Novakovic's research has led to her growing working facial bones. "We're now able to grow a full-size jawbone or cheekbone within three weeks," she says. She hopes these will be especially helpful for children, who need smaller bones. Also, bones that have grown from the patient's own cells will probably cause fewer side effects.

Seeing the Light

*I*n the late 1990s, two BMEs in Australia wanted any electronic junk they could get their hands on. Stereos, televisions, toys, cars—they took it all. Then they tore it apart to get the electronic parts. These researchers did not have enough money to buy their own parts. They did have a vision, though: to give vision to other people. They wanted to make a **bionic** eye.

They had a lot of requirements for their eye. For example, if you drop a cell phone in the ocean, that is the end of that phone. It only takes a minute for the salt water to soak in and ruin the phone. The human body is filled with salt water. The researchers knew their artificial eye had to have components that would survive in that environment for 50 years. The material also had to be strong enough to last, but flexible enough to move.

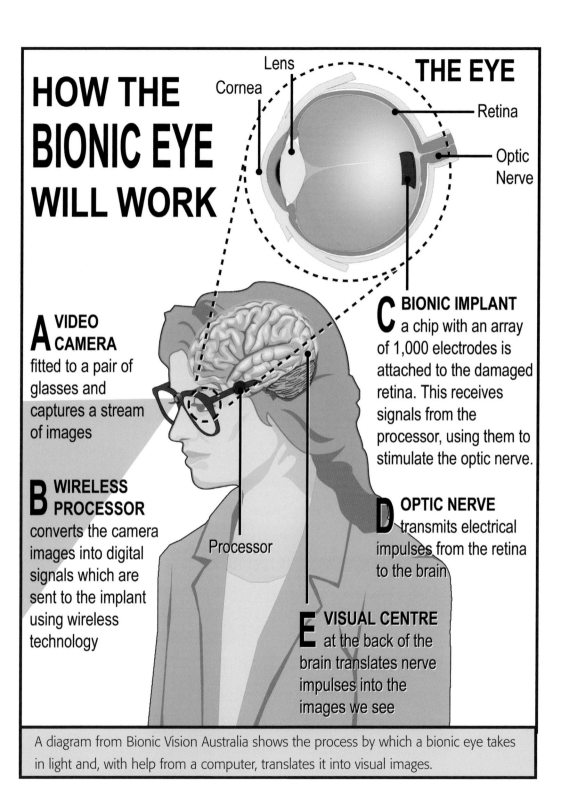

HOW THE BIONIC EYE WILL WORK

THE EYE

Cornea

Lens

Retina

Optic Nerve

A VIDEO CAMERA
fitted to a pair of glasses and captures a stream of images

B WIRELESS PROCESSOR
converts the camera images into digital signals which are sent to the implant using wireless technology

Processor

C BIONIC IMPLANT
a chip with an array of 1,000 electrodes is attached to the damaged retina. This receives signals from the processor, using them to stimulate the optic nerve.

D OPTIC NERVE
transmits electrical impulses from the retina to the brain

E VISUAL CENTRE
at the back of the brain translates nerve impulses into the images we see

A diagram from Bionic Vision Australia shows the process by which a bionic eye takes in light and, with help from a computer, translates it into visual images.

People with vision problems can wear the glasses and vastly improve their sight. The black disk at the left holds a tiny camera and sensor that tracks light and objects and feeds information to the system.

The way humans see is somewhat like a relay race. First, visual information (the things you see) goes to the **retina**. The retina senses light, colors, and shapes. The retina then delivers this information to the optic nerve—a kind of visual freeway that goes straight to the brain. Then the brain takes over. It reconstructs the information into the sights that we see.

In a bionic eye, a patient wears a pair of glasses with a camera attached. Then, doctors implant a small, electronic chip into the patient's retina. The glasses send visual information to the chip. The chip is tiny—only about two-by-four millimeters. (This capital letter "E" is about the size of the chip.) Even so, it can carry millions of signals.

People who get the bionic eye cannot see perfectly. Instead, the images look like groups of white dots in various shapes. It's just the first step, however. Dr. Nigel Lovell is one of the BMEs who worked on the project. He hopes the eye will eventually let people be able to tell faces apart. It's a lot of tough science. Lovell says, "I think to create a bionic eye is equivalent to trying to create a television as opposed to a radio."

The field of biomedical engineering is always changing. A doctor's office or hospital is equipped with dozens of useful devices. Many of them were once considered impossible to make, but there were a few dedicated BMEs who worked to turn dreams into realities. Today's BMEs are still busy imagining, designing, and building. The dreams of today will be the breakthrough technologies of tomorrow.

 **Text-Dependent Questions**

1. How is an exoskeleton different from a regular skeleton?
2. What does the retina in the eye do?
3. What were the three requirements for the internal bandage?

Research Project

Go to the drawing board! Come up with an idea for your own BME device or technique. What problem will it solve? Don't worry if you can't make it work yet. Right now you're just coming up with ideas.

Scientists in the News

Herman Schwan

Born in 1919 in Germany, Herman Schwan is sometimes called the "Father of Biomedical Engineering." When he began working in 1937, only a handful of people worked in the same field. Because he was Jewish, Schwan faced trouble in Nazi Germany during World War II. He came to the United States, where he established a BME department at the University of Pennsylvania. For one of his first projects, he studied how loud sounds affect human hearing. This led to the development of ear protection for people working around noisy machines such as airplanes. Schwan was always interested in how to make science helpful and practical to people. "Don't just observe properties," he said. "You must understand what's going on."

Robert Langer

When Robert Langer was 11, his parents gave him a chemistry set. He set up his first laboratory in the basement of his house and set to work. He made homemade rubber. He experimented with making things turn different colors. Today, Langer has another lab at the MIT, where he is a successful BME. In his work, Langer has studied long strings of molecules called polymers. He worked to figure out how these molecules could be used to deliver medicine into people's bodies. He has also designed polymers that can be covered with human cells. These cells then grow into new tissues that form bones or organs. Langer says, "I had this dream of using my background in chemistry and chemical engineering to improve people's lives."

Carlos Angulos Barrios

Dr. Barrios and his team at the University of Madrid in Spain came up with a way to attach very tiny sensors to human skin. They used nanotechnology, that is, making materials with almost microscopic parts. Sensors on people are nothing new, but the Madrid team's new method makes them smaller than ever and able to stick to uneven surfaces such as skin. The sensors can measure temperature, blood pressure, and breathing patterns. The method they used is very similar to how CDs are made, laying thin layers of material on a hard surface. Patients might not be able to see the tiny sensors, but they'll be working to help keep people healthy.

BME Robert Langer at his MIT office.

Find Out More

Books

Fullick, Ann. *Medical Technology*. Mankato, Minn.: Raintree, 2012.

Jango-Cohen, Judith. *Bionics*. Minneapolis: Lerner, 2006.

Johnson, Rebecca. *Nanotechnology*. Minneapolis: Lerner, 2005.

Parks, Deborah. *Nature's Machines: The Story of Biomechanist Mimi Koehl*. Washington, D.C.: Joseph Henry Press, 2006.

Web Sites

American Institute of Mechanical and Biological Engineering
navigate.aimbe.org/
Visit the site of a national organization of BMEs.

Science Buddies
www.sciencebuddies.org/science-engineering-careers/health/
biomedical-engineer#whatdotheydo
Learn more about the steps needed to become a BME.

Series Glossary of Key Terms

airlock   a room on a space station from which astronauts can move from inside to outside the station and back

anatomy   a branch of knowledge that deals with the structure of organisms

bionic   to be assisted by mechanical movements

carbon dioxide   a gas that is in the air that we breathe out

classified   kept secret from all but a few people in a government or an organization

deforestation   the destruction of forest or woodland

diagnose   to recognize by signs and symptoms

discipline   in science, this means a particular field of study

elite   the part or group having the highest quality or importance

genes   information stored in cells that determine a person's physical characteristics

geostationary   remaining in the same place above the Earth during an orbit

innovative   groundbreaking, original

inquisitiveness   an ability to be curious, to continue asking questions to learn more

internships   jobs often done for free by people in the early stages of study for a career

marine   having to do with the ocean

meteorologist   a scientist who forecasts weather and weather patterns

physicist   a scientist who studies physics, which examines how matter and energy move and relate

primate   a type of four-limbed mammal with a developed brain; includes humans, apes, and monkeys

traits   a particular quality or personality belonging to a person

Index

Photo Credits

About the Author

Diane Bailey has written about forty nonfiction books for kids and teens, on topics ranging from science to sports to celebrities. She is particularly interested in learning about how breakthroughs in science and technology are continually changing how people live. Diane also works as a freelance editor, usually from a chair in her living room in Kansas. She has two sons, two dogs, and some unidentified organisms living in the refrigerator.